Beyond The Far Side

Other Books in The Far Side Series

The Far Side
In Search of The Far Side
Bride of The Far Side
Valley of The Far Side
It Came From The Far Side
Hound of The Far Side
The Far Side Observer
Night of the Crash-Test Dummies
Wildlife Preserves
Wiener Dog Art
Unnatural Selections
Cows of Our Planet
The Chickens Are Restless
The Curse of Madame "C"

Anthologies

The Far Side Gallery
The Far Side Gallery 2
The Far Side Gallery 3
The Far Side Gallery 4
The Far Side Gallery 5

Retrospective

The PreHistory of The Far Side
 A 10th Anniversary Exhibit

BEYOND THE FAR SIDE

by GARY LARSON

Andrews and McMeel
A Universal Press Syndicate Company
Kansas City

ISBN: 0-8362-1149-9

Library of Congress Catalog Card Number: 83-71765

First Printing, August 1983
Thirty-third Printing, March 1996

Printed on recycled paper.

"Let's see . . . I guess your brother's coming over too . . . Better give it one more shake."

"Well, for crying out loud! . . . It's Uncle Irwin from the city sewer!"

"All right, Billy, you just go right ahead! . . . I've
warned you enough times about playing under the
anvil tree!"

6

"Well, well, King . . . looks like the new neighbors have brought a friend for you, too."

"I'm sorry, Irwin . . . It's your breath. It's . . . it's fresh and minty."

"Now wait just a minute here . . . How are we supposed to know you're the REAL Angel of Death?"

"Wait a minute! Say that again, Doris! . . . You know, the part about, 'If only we had some means of climbing down.'"

8

"Well, I dunno . . . Okay, sounds good to me."

"Hello, Emily. This is Gladys Murphy up the street.
Fine, thanks . . . Say, could you go to your window
and describe what's in my front yard?"

The African rhino: An animal with little or no sense
of humor

"I'm sorry, but we haven't any room . . . You'll have to sleep in the house."

"No, no, no! Now, try it again! . . . Remember, this
is our one and only ticket out of here!"

"Now don't you kids forget . . . Stay away from
old Mr. Weatherby's place."

Click!

"Focus! . . . Focus!"

"Well, here they come . . . You locked the keys inside, you do the talkin'."

My dinner with Andy

The duck relays

"Criminy! . . . It seems like every summer there's more and more of these things around!"

"Sandwiches!"

16

Young Jimmy Frankenstein

"Blast it, Henry! . . . I think the dog is following us."

In the days before television

"Down in front! . . . Sit down! . . . Sit down!"

Late at night, and without permission, Reuben would often enter the nursery and conduct experiments in static electricity.

"Listen out there! We're George and Harriet Miller! We just dropped in on the pigs for coffee! We're coming out! . . . We don't want trouble!"

"Just jump, fool! . . . You don't have to go,
'Boing, boing, boing!'"

"So, then . . . Would that be 'us the people' or
'we the people?'"

20

"General! Quick! Look! . . . Henderson is doing it again!"

Professor E. F. Gizmo and some of his many inventions

"Excuse me, but the others sent me up here to
ask you not to roll around so much."

"Step on it, Arnold! Step on it!"

23

"Say . . . Now I'M starting to feel kinda warm!"

"You know, we're just not reaching that guy."

"I say fifty, maybe a hundred horses . . . What you say, Red Eagle?"

"The golden arches! The golden arches got me!"

"Look! Look, gentlemen! . . . Purple mountains! Spacious skies! Fruited plains! . . . Is someone writing this down?"

Inevitably, their affair ended: Howard worried excessively about what the pack would think, and Agnes simply ate the flowers.

"And now there go the Wilsons! . . . Seems like everyone's evolving except us!"

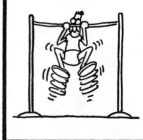

"One!"

"Listen . . . You go tell Billy's mother, and I'll
start looking for another old tire."

"And notice, gentlemen, the faster I go, the
more Simmons sounds like a motorboat."

"Mom! Dad! . . . The nose fairy left me a whole quarter!"

Things that go bump in the night

"Uh-oh, Lorraine . . . Someone seems to be checking you out."

"Do you know me? I have to deal with lions, wolves, and saber toothed tigers . . . That's why I carry one of THESE."

The embarrassment of "morning face"

"Freeze! . . . Okay, now . . . Who's the brains of this outfit?"

"Good heavens, Stuart! . . . We're going to need the net!"

"Now here comes the barbaric finale."

"NOW, you've got him, Vinnie!"

"The fool! . . . He's on the keyboard!"

"So, Mr. Fenton . . . Let's begin with your mother."

"Well, Emily is out like a light . . . Just can't resist pulling that little stunt of yours, can you, Earl!"

"Satisfied? . . . I warned you not to invite the cows in for a few drinks."

35

"We're too late! . . . He jumped!"

"Shhhh, Zog! . . . Here come one now!"

And then, from across the room, their eyes met.

"Yeeeeeeeeeeeha!"

38

"Now take them big birds, Barnaby . . . Never
eat a thing . . . Just sit and stare."

"Aaaaaaaaa! Murray! . . . A spider was in my shoe!"

"Knock it off, I said! . . . This is a still life!"

"Now on to other business . . . Ole Johnson here
has a new helmet design to show us!"

40

"Oooooooooooooool"

"Ha! The idiots spelled 'surrender' with only one 'r'!"

"Hey! They're lighting their arrows! . . . Can they DO that?"

"This is your side of the family, you realize."

"Hang on, Betty . . . Someone's bound to see us eventually."

"Blasted recoil unit!"

"Say . . . Look what THEY'RE doing."

"Shhhhhhh . . . I wanna surprise the kids."

"Rub his belly, Ernie! Rub his belly!"

"Let's see — Mosquitos, gnats, flies, ants . . .
What the? . . . Those jerks! We didn't order stink
bugs on this thing!"

"Well, I guess both Warren and the cat are okay
. . . But thank goodness for the Heimlich
maneuver!"

"Now don't forget, Gorok! . . . THIS time punch
some holes in the lid!"

"Stop the swing! I'm getting sick! Stop the swing! Oongowa! Oongowa!"

"Arnold, it's Mr. Wimberly on the phone . . . He says the next time you buzz his house, he'll have his 12-gauge ready."

"Wait! Wait! Listen to me! . . . We don't HAVE to be just sheep!"

"Why . . . yes . . . thank . . . you . . . I . . . would . . . like . . . a . . . knuckle . . . sandwich."

"Ha! We got him now!"

"Oh! Is that so? . . . Well, YOU'VE got a big MOUTH!"

"Good heavens, Ronald! . . . I think something landed on the roof!"

"I'm sorry, Margaret, but it's time I spread my wings and said goodbye."

"Well, once again, here we are."

"Say . . . Wait just a dang minute, here . . . We forgot the cattle!"

54

" 'Looks like a trap,' I said. 'Nonsense,' you said. 'No one would set a trap way out here in the woods,' you said."

"Try to relax, ma'am . . . You say it was dark;
you were alone in the house, when suddenly
you felt a hand reaching from behind and . . .
JOHNSON! Knock it off!"

"YOU, Bernie Horowitz? . . . So YOU'RE the
'they' in 'that's what they say'?"

55

"I just don't like it, Al . . . Whenever Billy goes outside, the new neighbors seem compelled to watch every little thing he does."

"All right! All right! I confess! I did it! Yes! That's right! The cow! Ha ha ha! And I feel great!"

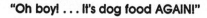

"Oh boy! . . . It's dog food AGAIN!"

The rare and timid prairie people

"He was magnificent! Just magnificent! And I almost had him! . . . I can't talk about it right now."

"We're the Wilsons, bozo! What's it say on the box?"

"Well, you can just rebuild the fort later, Harold . . . Phyllis and Shirley are coming over and I'll need the cushions."

"The cape, Larry! Go for the cape!"

"You boys gotta bottle-opener?"

"See, Barbara? There's no one in here, no one outside . . . I'll even open the drapes and have a look."

"Now wait a minute . . . He said two jerks means 'more slack' and three meant 'come up' . . . but he never said nothin' about one long, steady pull."

Car key gnomes

"Pull out, Betty! Pull out! . . . You've hit an artery!"

"Ha! Webster's blown his cerebral cortex."

The real reason dinosaurs became extinct

"I'm not warning you again, Sparky! . . . You chew with your mouth OPEN!"

"All right! Rusty's in the club!"

Metamorphosis

"Say, Thag . . . Wall of ice closer today?"

"Well, for goodness sakes! . . . What is this thing?"

"Rapunzel, Rapunzel! . . . Let down your hair!"

"That was incredible. No fur, claws, horns,
antlers, or nothin' . . . Just soft and pink."

"Well, well . . . Looks like it's time for the old luggage test."

"Well, don't bring the filthy things in here, you imbecile! . . . Take 'em down to the lake!"

"Fool! This is an eleven-sixteenths . . . I asked
for a five-eighths!"

"Well, look who's here . . . God's gift to
wart hogs."

With a reverberating crash, Lulu's adventure on the tractor had come to an abrupt end.

"For heaven's sake! Harold! Wake up! We've got bed buffaloes!"

72

"I . . . could . . . have . . . sworn . . . you . . .
said . . . eleven . . . steps."

Evolution of the Stickman

73

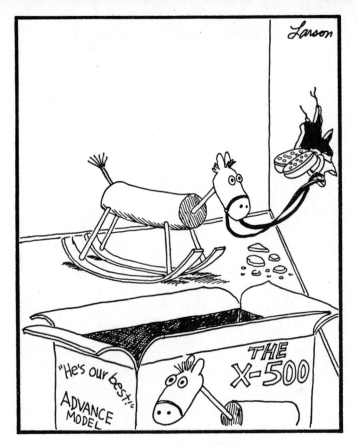

"Okay, here we go! Remember, wiggle those noses, stuff those cheeks, and act cute — and no smoking, Carl."

"Say . . . Now THERE'S a little hat!"

"My project's ready for grading, Mr. Big Nose
. . . Hey! I'm talkin' to YOU, squidbrain!"

"You know? . . . I think I'd like a salad."

"Say . . . What's a mountain goat doing way up here in a cloud bank?"

"Neanderthals, Neanderthals! Can't make fire!
Can't make spear! Nyah, nyah, nyah . . . !"

Lewis and Clark meet Sylvia and Rhonda.

"Freeze, Earl! Freeze! . . . Something rattled!"

Animals and their mating songs

"Three wishes? Did I say three wishes? . . .
Shoot! I'll grant you FOUR wishes."

"Again? Oh, all right . . . One warm, summer evening many years ago, I was basking on a stretch of Interstate 95 not far from here . . ."

"What? . . . They turned it into a WASTEbasket?"

81

"Well, just look at you, Jimmy! . . . Soaking wet, hair mussed up, shoes untied . . . and take that horrible thing out of your mouth!"

"What did I say, Boris? . . . These new uniforms are a crock!"

Brian has a rendezvous with destiny.

"Well, here comes Stanley now . . . Good heavens! What's he caught THIS time?"

"It worked! It worked!"

"Not too close, Higgins . . . This one's got a knife."

"Whoa! . . . That CAN'T be right!"

"Well, why don't you come up here and MAKE me turn it down . . . or do you just TALK big, fellah?"

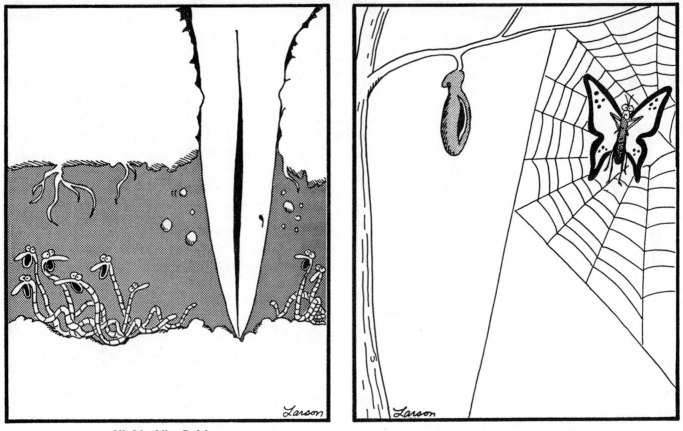

Night of the Robin

Life in the petri dish

"Okay! Now don't move, Andy! Here comes Mom!"

"How cute, Earl . . . The kids have built a little fort in the backyard."

"Blast! Up to now, the rhino was one of my prime suspects."

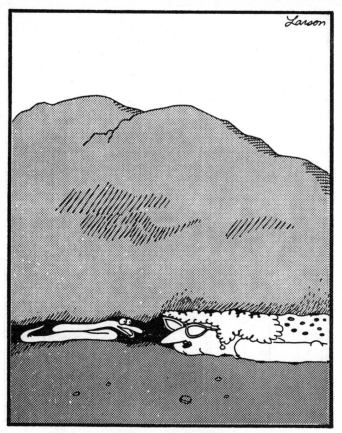

"It's true, Barbara . . . You're the first woman
I've ever brought here."

89

"YOU again!"

Cow philosophy

"You've got to watch out for them gopher holes, Roger."

"Kids! Kids! . . . The slugs are back!"

"You guys are both witnesses . . . He laughed
when my marshmallow caught fire."

During the night, and as yet unbeknownst to
Zelda, Phil had installed a volume knob.

94

"Calm down, Edna . . . Yes, it's some giant, hideous insect . . . but it could be some giant, hideous insect in need of help."

"Sol . . . You must be the one they call 'The Kid.'"

"What a find, Williams! The fossilized footprint
of a brachiosaurus! . . . And a Homo habilus
thrown in to boot!"

"I've got it again, Larry . . . an eerie feeling like
there's something on top of the bed."

"By the way, we're playing cards with the Millers tonight . . . And Edna says if you promise not to use your X-ray vision, Warren promises not to bring his Kryptonite."

"Wouldn't you know it! . . . And always just before a big date!"

"The name is Bill . . . Buffalo Bill."

"Hey! You! . . . No cutting in!"

"Well, little Ahab . . . Which one is it going to be?"

"And the murderer is . . . THE BUTLER! Yes, the butler . . . Who, I'm convinced, first gored the Colonel to death before trampling him to smithereens."

"I wouldn't do that, mister . . . Old Zeek's liable
to fire that sucker up."

"Well, good heavens! . . . I can't believe you
men . . . I'VE got some rope!"

"What did I say, Alex? . . . Every time we invite the Zombies over, we all end up just sitting around staring at each other."

104